Drought

Catherine Chambers

Heinemann
LIBRARY

www.heinemann.co.uk
Visit our website to find out more information about Heinemann Library books.

To order:
 Phone 44 (0) 1865 888066
 Send a fax to 44 (0) 1865 314091
Visit the Heinemann Bookshop at www.heinemann.co.uk to browse our catalogue and order online.

First published in Great Britain by Heinemann Library, Halley Court, Jordan Hill, Oxford OX2 8EJ
a division of Reed Educational and Professional Publishing Ltd. Heinemann is a registered trademark of Reed Educational & Professional Publishing Ltd.

OXFORD MELBOURNE AUCKLAND JOHANNESBURG BLANTYRE
GABORONE IBADAN PORTSMOUTH (NH) USA CHICAGO

Designed by Celia Floyd
Originated by Dot Gradations
Printed by Wing King Tong, in Hong Kong

04 03 02 01 00
10 9 8 7 6 5 4 3 2 1

ISBN 0 431 09603 1

British Library Cataloguing in Publication Data

Chambers, Catherine
Drought. – (Disasters in Nature)
1. Droughts – Juvenile literature
I. Title
551.5'773

Acknowledgements

The Publishers would like to thank the following for permission to reproduce photographs:

Ardea: Adrian Warren pg.23, P Morris pg.18; *Bruce Coleman Collection*: Fred Bruemmer pg.22, pg.41, Hans Reinhard pg.28, Peter Davey pg.34; *Environmental Images*: James de Bounevialle pg.33; *FLPA*: B Borrell pg.16, Roger Tidman pg.21; *Hulton Getty*: pg.40; *Hutchinson Library*: Brinicombe pg.11; *Images of Africa Photobank*: Dominic Harcourt Webster pg.6; *NHPA*: Christophe Ratier pg.42, John Shaw pg.24, pg.27, Nigel J Dennis pg.26, T Kitchen & V Hurst pg.17; *Panos*: pg.39, Jeremy Hartley pg.8, Liba Taylor pg.9, Penny Tweedie pg.35; *Photri*: Richard T Nowitz pg.43; *Planet Earth Pictures*: David Kjaer pg.29, Ford Kristo pg.45, John Downer pg.14; *Still Pictures*: Heine Pedersen pg.38, Mark Edwards pg.25; *Tony Stone*: Alan R Moller pg.44, Larry Ulrich pg.13, Thierry Boredon pg.31; *Tropix*: J Woollard pg.36.

Cover photograph reproduced with permission of Robert Harding Picture Library.

Our thanks to Mandy Barker for her comments in the preparation of this book.

Every effort has been made to contact copyright holders of any material reproduced in this book. Any omissions will be rectified in subsequent printings if notice is given to the Publisher.

Any words appearing in the text in bold, **like this**, are explained in the Glossary.

Contents

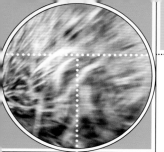

Introduction

What is drought?

Drought is caused by an unusually long period without a supply of water. Sometimes it occurs because rain has not fallen for several years. Rivers and streams stop flowing. Water in dams **evaporates**. Underground supplies of water run out. Crops dry out. The lives of humans, animals and plants are seriously threatened. Drought becomes a natural disaster.

Where does drought strike?

As the map shows, drought occurs mostly in deserts and in the naturally hot parts of the world. Drought disasters usually happen where a hot, dry climate affects the world's poorest people who struggle to feed themselves and who have little choice but to use the land in the way they do. Poverty creates political instability. This often results in war, which makes those affected by natural drought even worse off.

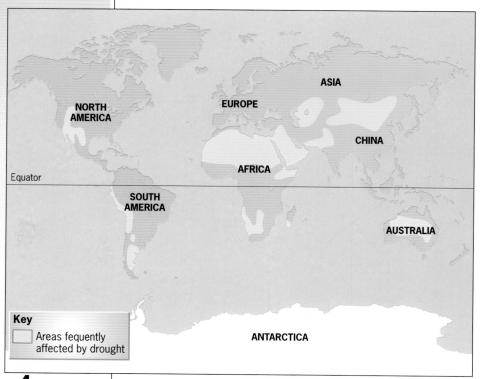

ASIA

EUROPE

NORTH
AMERICA

CHINA

Equator

AFRICA

SOUTH
AMERICA

AUSTRALIA

ANTARCTICA

Key

Areas frequently
affected by drought

This map shows the world's main drought zones. They include the most obvious places – the vast expanses of desert. Around the edges of the desert, drought comes and goes so it cannot be mapped accurately.

Drought data

- **Permanent drought** occurs in dry desert regions. Rainfall is rare and farming depends on artificial **irrigation**.

- **Seasonal drought** is a feature of places which are very dry for most of the year, with a short rainy season.

- **Contingent drought** is experienced when the rainy season is cut short, produces very little rain or does not arrive at all.

- **Unpredictable drought** is found in areas where rainbursts can be quite heavy but cannot be predicted.

- **Invisible drought** is the effect of scanty rainfall which harms crops and wildlife but does not completely destroy them.

Drought in our hands

Drought is often caused by a change in weather patterns and climate, but these do not always occur naturally. Some people believe that drought due to **global warming** is caused by human activity. Drought can also occur when water is made unavailable by what people do. For example, farmers may build channels or dams and underground pipes to take water for crops, drying out river beds, lakes, wetlands and underground water supplies.

Drought on our minds

Our growing cities, industry and agriculture use a lot of water. Until we take drought seriously, methods of saving water and using it carefully will never become natural to us. We shall always carelessly leave the tap running! We only take notice of drought when it affects us, or when we see disturbing images of disasters in the news.

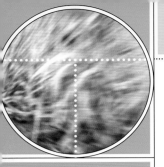

Drought disaster in the Sahel

A living hell

In 1985, the rest of the world was shocked by the tragedy of seeing feeding centres and refugee camps in Ethiopia that were sheltering millions of starving people. This was a horrific result of war on top of a drought disaster that had devastated many parts of the African **Sahel** since 1969. During 1984 and 1985 alone, nearly a million people died from starvation and disease. Wars and conflict in Ethiopia, Sudan, Somalia and Uganda had added to natural disaster, which some scientists have blamed on **global warming** and **El Niño**. Refugees walked hundreds of kilometres, first from drought-stricken Ethiopia to Somalia and the Sudan, and then back again as drought hit those areas, too.

Drought data

- The edge of the Sahara moves southwards 5 kilometres (3 miles) every year into the Sahel.

- Lake Chad has shrunk from 17 800 square kilometres (6900 square miles) to 3900 square kilometres (1500 square miles) in the last 20 years.

- In 1973, 80 per cent of livestock in Mauritania died as a result of drought in the Sahel.

Thousands of refugees struck by famine rely on food distributed through massive aid projects like this one in Ethiopia.

Where and why did it happen?

Although the word Sahel means 'coastal strip', it does not refer to a sea coast. Rather, it describes the fringe of the Sahara, the biggest desert in the world (and it's growing). As the map below shows, the Sahel region stretches across west and central Africa just south and east of the Sahara. It has also come to include the dry countries on the eastern edge of the desert. The Sahel is very dry between October and June but in normal years it has a short season of rainfall between June and September. This is enough to grow drought-resistant crops and raise animals but in recent times there have been three long periods of unpredictable rains causing **contingent drought** (see page 5). These occurred from 1969 to 1974, from the early to mid-1980s, and again in the early 1990s.

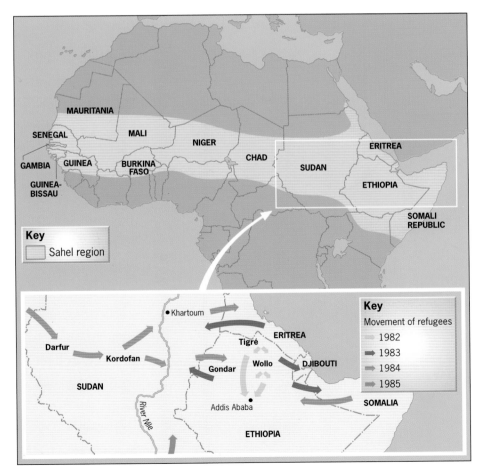

The map shows how people moved from one part of the Sahel to another to find food and shelter. This was partly due to war, which stopped many victims from staying in or returning to their own land.

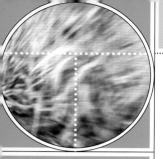

What have we learned?

Early warning – early reaction

People learned a lot from the **Sahel** drought disaster. Governments and aid agencies have developed better systems for predicting and dealing with natural disasters in fragile areas of the world.

- **Hazard mapping** can now forecast when drought is likely to happen in risk areas.
- Models calculated by computers predict disasters, based on how often and how widespread previous disasters hit a particular area.
- Data on population and **infrastructure** such as roads and communications are kept up to date.
- Food supplies and transport equipment are stockpiled and emergency plans are updated.

Traditional farming methods like this, which use no **irrigation**, are being encouraged by governments and aid agencies. Manure is mixed with soil and made into a crescent-shaped wall. Rainwater and dew collect around the wall. Seeds are then sown into the damp soil.

Drought data

- Traditionally, an area of farmland in the Sahel is cleared and cultivated for three years. The crops use up most of the **nutrients**, so the farmer leaves the land uncultivated for the following eight years. This allows natural plants to grow back, die and return nutrients and **humus** to the soil.

- Moisture **evaporates** from plants five times as slowly as it does from pools of standing water, so keeping vegetation helps to preserve moisture near the ground. Plants clustered together also protect soil from water loss.

Felling the forests – clearing the land

Clearing trees, shrubs and natural grasses in **semi-arid** areas has the same effect as letting animals **overgraze**. In many parts of the world, trees are cut down as fuel and timber for sale abroad. This causes serious soil erosion. In much of the Sahel there are no more trees left, so animal manure is mixed with straw, dried and used as fuel instead. This means that manure and straw stubble cannot be used to fertilize fields or provide humus which helps to retain moisture in the soil. Chemical fertilizers that are used to replace natural ones have no long-term benefits for soil and have to be bought every year. **Reforestation** programmes are now top priority in Ethiopia, which has cut down all but two per cent of its natural forest. Over the last ten years, 500 million trees have been planted.

Most people in the Sahel use either wood or charcoal-burning stoves. Cutting down trees or using precious straw and manure for fuel adds to soil erosion and drought problems. This is one of several new designs, which uses up less fuel than older stoves.

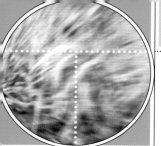

Shocking images

For several months, newspapers and news broadcasts were filled with images from feeding camps in the **Sahel**, but this was after three desperate years of drought, war and famine. After a British journalist 'discovered' the camp – and several more, all of which had been trying to cope with only a little help from the rest of the world – news reporters flocked to Ethiopia. They were quickly followed by a flurry of aid agencies, and foreign governments full of promises. Would this attention have been focused on the disaster if journalists had not reported it?

Selecting the story

Some governments are more open to publicity than others. During the mid-1980s media attention was focused on drought and starvation in Somalia and Ethiopia – but people in other parts of Africa were dying, too. Niger suffered drought disaster in 1984, as did Mauritania in 1983 and Burkina Faso in 1985. And altogether between 1968 and 1973, probably another half million people died as a result of famine and disease in other parts of the Sahel. And what about the 'developed' world? Rich nations experience drought disaster. Although human life is not threatened in the same way, millions of livestock, vast areas of crops and natural plants and countless animals often die.

Emergency aid

The international community responded to the famine in Ethiopia with high-profile fund-raising events, including the Live Aid pop concerts. At first, the £63 million (US $100 million) raised was used for emergency food aid. Because of war many people had nowhere to go to restart farming, so some of the money was used for longer-term projects to resettle communities and provide seeds and tools.

Comic Relief is a money-raising television appeal that takes place in Britain every two years. It came about after the 1984 drought disaster in the Horn of Africa. The main point of the campaign in 1999 was not just to raise money. It was also to highlight the problem of 'Third World' debt, which is money owed by poorer nations to rich countries and international banks. Paying back these loans cripples the economies of poor countries. Comic Relief has called upon all rich nations to cancel the debt, which would make poorer countries more self-sufficient, more politically stable and less likely to need help in the future.

In Great Britain, Red Nose Day aims not only to raise money for aid, but also to raise awareness about the money problems facing poor countries. Here English Comedian Lenny Henry (in hat) examines a new well in Uganda built using Red Nose Day contributions.

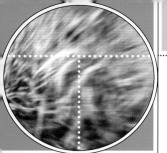

Weather watching

Hot spots

Drought disaster often occurs at the edges of deserts – the hottest, driest spots in the world. The map below shows where most of the world's deserts lie. Rain rarely falls in these areas as the air is nearly always dry. This is due to constant **high pressure**, which is an area of dry, dense, descending air. The air in a high pressure zone becomes more dense as it descends, and gets drier. It does not hold enough moisture to form clouds. Clouds usually form in warm, rising air, which cools high up. As clouds rise, the water vapour **condenses**, the droplets become heavier and eventually fall as rain. This is unlikely to happen in the desert regions.

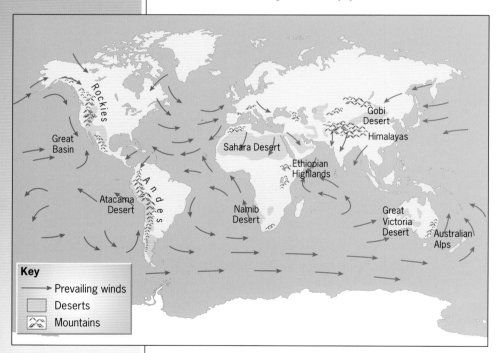

Key
→ Prevailing winds
☐ Deserts
⌇ Mountains

Not all deserts (left) are hot. There are cool and cold deserts, too. Most cold deserts lie on **plateaux**, high up between mountain ranges. It is their **altitude** that makes them cold. Nevertheless, both cool and cold deserts can be scorching during the day.

Cool currents

The map also shows that some of the deserts are on the west coasts of continents. This is because cold ocean currents cool the air above them. As it is warm, rising air that usually forms clouds, here the air is too cool to hold moisture. When these oceanic winds blow onto the land, they bring no rain with them.

Beyond the mountains

The map also shows that many deserts lie to the west of mountain ranges, in **rainshadow areas**. The Andes in South America, the Rockies in North America and the Great Dividing Range in Australia all stop rain from reaching the western deserts. The **prevailing winds** blow mostly over warm oceans, picking up lots of moisture as they go. The winds drive the moist air over the land. Most of it forms clouds and the water falls as rain before it reaches the mountains. The remaining moist air is forced upwards by the mountains. It cools as it rises, and the final rain falls on the near side of the mountain. By the time the air reaches the top of the mountain there is little or no moisture left.

Some deserts, such as the Mojave in the United States pictured here, are surrounded by mountains, so it does not matter which way the wind blows – the desert will get no rain. Some deserts, such as the Atacama in Chile, are affected by both cold ocean currents and by being in a rainshadow area. It finally rained in the Atacama in 1971 – after 400 years without a drop of water!

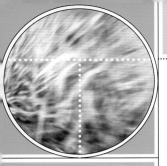

What brings the rain?

Rain is part of the **water cycle**. This is the way in which the Earth's supply of water is recycled all the time in different forms. Sometimes it is held in the air as invisible water vapour – sometimes it falls as rain, snow, sleet or hail. Most of it lies in massive oceans, seas and lakes, or it is held frozen in **ice sheets** and **glaciers**. Some flows as rivers and streams. There is always the same amount of water on the Earth, even if we cannot actually see all of it. The water cycle is a very fast global system. This makes it very difficult to predict accurately. But how does this system work?

Each river runs through a **catchment area**, from which all surface and underground water finds its way to just one river. Each catchment area lies in a **river basin**, which is divided from its neighbouring basin by higher ground known as a watershed. A river is fed not only by the streams that run into it but also by the water that seeps through the soil.

Sun, wind and rain

When the sun shines and the wind blows over the oceans, seas and great lakes, water **evaporates** from the surface. If the air above the body of water is warm it is able to hold a lot of vapour. If the air is warm it will rise. As warm, moist air rises the water vapour in it cools and **condenses**, and rain falls. Some rain falls on the oceans, but a lot falls on land. Clouds rise up hill and mountain slopes, shedding rain before they reach the other side. The drops fall down the slope, gathering together in streams. The streams flow into rivers, and the rivers into seas. The cycle begins all over again, but it is unpredictable. We never know in advance exactly where rain will fall – or how much.

Making rain

Chemicals or dust can be fired into a cloud to make the water droplets inside it condense and fall as raindrops. This is called seeding, and is sometimes used to save crops from shrivelling.

Drought data

Drought can be caused by a number of things. The main causes are listed below.

- **Aquifer drought** is caused by a shortage of **groundwater**, which means that plant roots find it difficult to reach a water source, topsoils dry out and are blown away by the wind.

- **Precipitation drought** is due to a lack of rainfall, which affects the surface of the ground and rivers immediately, and groundwater in the long term.

- **Run-off drought** is caused when surface running water, such as streams, rivulets and rivers dry out.

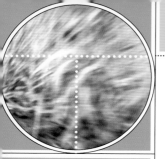

A natural change

Scientists agree that the climate generally has become warmer and drier over the last 10 000 years. This change has been happening since the last Ice Age began to retreat and **ice sheets**, **ice caps** and **glaciers** began to melt. The main reason for climatic change on such a scale during this time is how close the Earth is to the Sun. The distance between the Earth and the Sun varies slightly as we rotate in the solar system. The overall result is that the climate is warming and drying. There have been variations to this pattern along the way. These have included mini Ice Ages, wet phases and hot phases. There is evidence that one of these occurred between 1250 and 1700 CE – that's only 300 years ago. These small blips of extra-cold or extra-hot weather are called **oscillations**.

Global warming

It takes a difference of only 1–2° Celsius (1.8–3.6° Fahrenheit) to change the Earth's climate and weather patterns quite dramatically. It is thought that in 30 years' time, the world will be at least 1° Celsius (1.8° Fahrenheit) hotter. Many scientists believe that the rise in temperature is due to **global warming** caused largely by the release of certain gases into the atmosphere.

Each ring in a tree's trunk represents one year's growth. When the rings are close together, it means that the tree has not grown very fast. It has had to conserve moisture in order to survive. This means that there was probably drought at that time.

Since the beginning of the **Industrial Revolution** over 200 years ago, fossil fuels have been burned in massive quantities. At the same time, people have been using up trees, which absorb carbon dioxide from the air, so nature's ability to balance the gases has been disrupted.

Living in a greenhouse

Heat from the Sun is radiated to the Earth, which absorbs some of it and reflects or radiates some of it back towards space. The Earth is kept warm by a **greenhouse effect** as the **atmosphere** absorbs the reflected heat. An enhanced greenhouse effect is thought to be caused by **carbon gases** (released when we burn coal and oil in factories, power stations and houses), particularly carbon dioxide, rising into the atmosphere. These act like a mirror, reflecting the heat back down to Earth. This enhanced greenhouse effect raises the temperature of the air, sea and the land and could possibly lead to less rain falling in desert and semi-desert areas.

Scientists believe that further global warming is caused by the thinning of the **ozone layer** of gases in the atmosphere. Chlorofluorocarbon gases (**CFCs**) from refrigerators, aerosol cans and also volcanoes contain chlorine gas, which destroys ozone molecules.

17

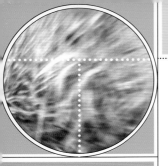

The effects of El Niño

El Niño is the name for one of the most devastating freak weather conditions in the world. El Niño was first noticed by fishermen from Peru, who experienced tempestuous storms at Christmas time. El Niño is thought to cause torrential rain and heavy flooding, violent hurricanes and terrifying tornadoes. It also brings weeks of record-breaking temperatures, high humidity, sudden drought and forest fires.

The power of El Niño

It seems strange that a single weather feature can have such different effects, but then, El Niño is a very strange feature! In the Pacific Ocean, it is marked by warmer ocean currents and the dramatic reversal of **prevailing winds** – winds that blow in roughly the same direction all year round. There is also thought to be a similar phenomenon in the atmosphere above the Atlantic Ocean. This change in air pressure and winds is called the **North Atlantic Oscillation** (NAO). It affects western Europe and North Africa and is thought to be responsible – among other things – for violent sandstorms in the Sahara.

The extreme heat and the drought brought by El Niño in 1998 helped to hatch out millions of mosquitoes in parts of South America. This brought high levels of **malaria**, an often fatal disease that is transmitted by mosquitoes. It increased cases of **dengue fever**, a virus also carried by mosquitoes.

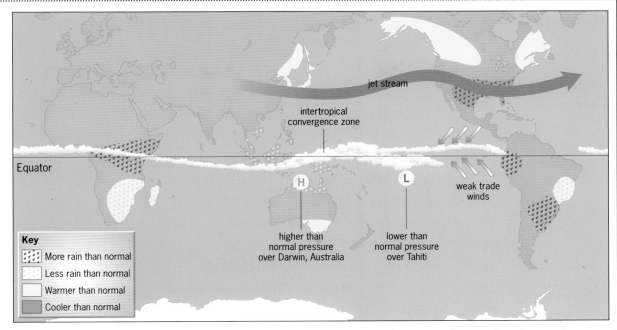

The map shows the dramatic, global, climatic effects of El Niño.

El Niños of the past

We can discover a lot about past El Niños by studying tree rings, soil sediments at the bottom of the ocean and cores from the thick ice at the poles. We can also use historical evidence such as written and spoken accounts of past climatic disasters. Together they reveal some surprising evidence, linking El Niño with plagues and famines, and crop failures.

Measuring the heat

Sudden extreme temperatures caused by El Niño can be deadly. In farming areas, plants wither and animals die very quickly. So, too, do humans, who suffer dehydration, breathing difficulties and heart attacks but, unlike drought disasters, human death occurs mostly in the cities, especially where there is heavy pollution. Death occurs particularly when humidity and temperatures are high and there is no breeze. The United States has created a 'heat index' which advises people when it is best to stay indoors or in the shade.

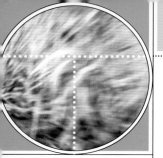

Another sunny day

What happens when there is no cloud cover? The most obvious thing is that there is no rain. Daylong sunshine withers plants and then scorches the bare, thin topsoils, which is where plants get most of their **nutrients**. In **semi-arid** lands all these effects cause problems for both **arable** and **pastoral farming** as well as for wild plants and animals. They also affect **irrigated** land that has been reclaimed for agriculture. Pumped-up **groundwater** has salts and minerals in it that have been dissolved from underground rock. When the sun dries out the surface, a salty or **alkaline** crust is left, which makes conditions difficult for plant life.

Soils in hot places

Moisture helps to create soil, and work with micro-organisms to break down dead plants into a rich topsoil called **humus**. Deserts have very little moisture and few plants, so soils do not develop easily.

In Africa there are many areas of dry, tropical grasslands known as **savannah**. In the long dry season, savannah vegetation dies back and forms a rich layer of humus. Moisture and minerals are drawn up to the surface. The Sun then **evaporates** surface moisture and bakes the minerals into a hard, red crust. For the natural savannah plants, this is not too much of a problem, as eventually they decay again into a rich humus. Cultivating this soil is another matter, as the surface is often very hard to plough.

Temperate grasslands include the pampas of South America, the **prairies** of Mid-West America and the Australian Murray-Darling grasslands west of the Great Dividing Range. Their grasses have a very thick network of roots and these, together with the grass blades, decay during winter into a rich protective layer.

These grassland soils are very dark in colour and are known as black earths or **chernozems**. They are really quite fertile. The plants that live in them have adapted to survive several years of drought.

In China, the heavy monsoon rains wash away about 1.5 billion tonnes of a yellow clay-like soil called loess each year.

Drought data

- One centimetre (0.4 inches) of soil on the **loess plateau** of North China is washed away every year. This soil loss has been caused by deforestation (tree felling) and ploughing up grassland for intensive farming. This is the fastest rate of soil loss in the world.

- Seventy per cent of soil erosion in the United States is caused by human action. Dramatic climatic changes and intensive agriculture have made the prairies a drought disaster several times this century. The worst occurred in the 1930s. The prairies turned into a dustbowl and led to the migration of thousands of impoverished and malnourished farmers. Since then, millions of trees have been planted to reduce erosion.

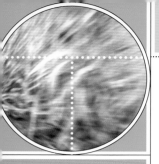

Plants in dry climates

Why does natural plant growth succeed in dry lands, where cultivation by humans often fails so miserably? Many plant species have evolved over thousands of years to survive and even thrive in dry conditions.

Tough trees

In **semi-arid** areas, trees are **xerophytic**, which means they have developed resistance to drought. Trees in dry places have developed small, waxy leaves to slow down moisture loss through their **stomata**. Some trees have thorny leaves, so that there is very little surface area exposed to the Sun. Roots often spread deep and wide to catch as much moisture as possible. Trunks have thick bark to prevent dew and moisture from **evaporating**. The **savannah** acacia and the Australian eucalyptus trees have wide-spreading branches which form a shady canopy to conserve moisture beneath them. Other trees are **pyrophytic**, which means they are able to resist forest fire.

This salt-bush is a **halophyte**. Halophytes are plants that have adapted to the high levels of salt and other chemicals often found in desert and semi-desert soils. They manage to carry excess chemicals in the sap and transport them to the leaves, where they are let out through tiny holes.

Many trees of **arid** regions have edible fruit. The date palm, often found near oases, has to cope with blistering sun, salty soil and dry winds, as well as freezing nights. It provides a fruit that can be dried and easily transported. The baobab tree grows in semi-arid areas in Africa, Australia and other parts of the world. They are both xerophytic and pyrophytic. In Africa, the thick, spongy trunk of the baobab is used to store water and the inner bark is made into rope. The fruit pulp is made into a drink and the leaves are dried and ground into a powder that can be cooked into a vegetable sauce.

Protected plants

Most cacti have swollen stems which help them to store water for a long time. The thick, waxy surface prevents moisture loss and the stems are shaped so that when the sudden rains come the water rolls straight towards the roots. The cacti's huge root system spreads out to absorb as much water as possible. Some cacti have spines, which are really leaves which have evolved to lose very little moisture and to protect them from being eaten by plant-eating animals.

Tropical savannah grasses have slim, sword-like blades topped with silky flower spikes. The blades are bunched together in protective, water-saving tufts. The grasses grow over 3 metres (10 feet) tall and shoot up quickly during the summer rains.

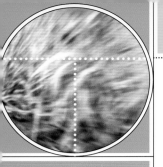

Choosing crops

All over the world and for thousands of years farmers have tried to grow crops in **arid** regions. The most successful farmers have chosen drought-resistant crops, using only rain, dew and any **groundwater** that the plants' roots can draw up for themselves. Some have also used the natural seasonal flooding of rivers to plant crops which grow and ripen before the flooded land dries out. The least successful have grown more fragile crops needing **irrigated** water in order to survive.

Beans have been planted in between the cereal crop, a method known as **inter-cropping**. The beans will ripen later than the cereal and so will hold the soil together, and also keep in moisture. When bean plants wither, they return **nutrients** to the soil.

Growing grains

Millet and sorghum are small-grained cereals that are well adapted to very dry conditions. They have waxy stalks and leaves which allow very little water to **evaporate** from them. The tiny seeds are also protected by a tough outer skin to prevent water loss. Millet and sorghum are grown extensively in the **Sahel**, while millet is also a major crop in India. Seeds are sown at the onset of the rains and in normal years manage to grow and ripen on the scanty rain from showers.

On the Canadian **prairies** and the Great Plains of the United States, faster-growing drought and disease-resistant varieties of wheat and maize are cultivated. Unlike the millet and sorghum of the Sahel, American crops are treated relentlessly with fertilizers and pesticides which can, in the long term, damage water sources and the environment. Neither of these crops can survive solely on rainwater, unless it is a particularly wet year. Groundwater is pumped up to irrigate them, which means underground water supplies are lost much more quickly than can be replaced by rain, so the water table goes increasingly lower.

Crops that require a lot of sunshine to ripen are not necessarily drought-resistant. One of these is cotton, which is grown in the dry state of Texas. Cotton requires a lot more water than wheat or maize and needs irrigation, so it is probably not the best crop to grow, but farmers are given **subsidies** (extra money) by the government to produce it. This is because it can be exported, which brings money into the country.

Sorghum is well adapted to very dry conditions, and provides an essential crop to these farmers in Burkina Faso.

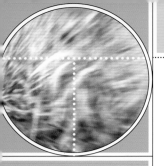

Animals in dry climates

Rearing animals in **semi-arid** lands is the least profitable type of farming for the amount of land used. This is because of the huge area of land required for grazing and the large amount of time and effort put in by the farmworker. Most sheep and cattle are herded over vast areas of cheap land with just enough grass to feed and fatten them. In normal years this works satisfactorily, but during times of drought, in areas such as central Australia, farmers have to give their animals extra food, which has to be grown by the farmer or bought in. This is an added expense, which multiplies the effects of drought on farming families.

The right kind of cattle

Domestic animals such as goats, sheep and cattle can be carefully bred to suit dry conditions. The Pampas regions of Uruguay and northern Argentina are cattle country. The animals roam over huge ranches, some of them spreading over 100 square kilometres (about 40 square miles). These cattle were originally a local variety, which were then bred with European bulls to improve the strength and quality of the animal, and also bred with the Asian Brahman bull, which allowed the cattle to withstand the hot, dry conditions.

This male African sandgrouse is well adapted to dry conditions. It will fly 50 kilometres (about 30 miles) to the nearest oasis to find water for its chicks. It fluffs out its under-feathers on the water so that the feathers soak it up. The chicks can then suck out the water.

The Masai of Kenya and Tanzania skilfully puncture the veins of cattle and drain some of the blood. This provides a rich source of iron and other **nutrients** without killing the animal. If you watch this practice, you will see that the cattle do not seem alarmed at what is happening to them.

The ship of the desert

The camel is known as the 'ship of the desert' and, since ancient times, has been used to transport goods and people across both hot and cold deserts. One of the most important goods carried by the camel across the Sahara is salt, which in hot climates is vital to balance moisture in the human body. The ancient salt mines of Bilma are still working, and the camels are still transporting salt cakes across the desert as they have done for hundreds of years.

The camel is also an important source of food. Each female camel is able to provide 30 litres (63 US pints) of milk a day in good conditions. Camels can provide meat as well, although for traders, it is often seen as a waste of a good pack animal. Camels can drink huge amounts of water and then survive for many days without touching a drop. Camels also store fat in their humps, which their bodies use up when food is scarce.

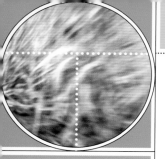

Drought disaster in the natural world

Winners and losers

Not all plants can survive in drought conditions. We have seen how tough grasses can resist the hot sun and the drying wind. But grasses in cooler climates lose moisture rapidly through the **stomata** in their thin blades. Their roots do not go down far enough in the soil to tap into low-lying **groundwater**. As the ground dries out they just shrivel up, although seeds can lie in the soil for several years until rain swells them and they produce new grass shoots. Wild flower seeds can also survive in the same way.

Vultures are scavengers that can take advantage of drought conditions by feeding on the many animal **carcasses** strewn around the parched landscape.

Wetland plants cannot cope with dry conditions at all, and wetland areas are slow to recover following drought. Waterlilies and other similar plants take in a lot of moisture and minerals through their thick, twisted roots, or through many slender tendrils that hang from their stems. Their leaves are adapted to losing moisture – not conserving it. Thousands of tiny holes allow the water to **evaporate** so that the plant does not rot. Many water plants produce floating seed capsules, which have no way of dispersing if the water is too shallow and too still. Tiny algae die in their millions during a drought. These are normally food for small freshwater creatures, which in turn are eaten by larger fish. Mammals such as the otter and the mink then feed on the fish. By killing the algae, drought affects the whole chain of natural water life.

One of the richest marshlands in Europe is the Côta Doñana on the southern coast of Spain. It is a stopping place for migrating birds such as the pink flamingo. Some of its margins have been drained to build holiday apartments and to **irrigate** nearby strawberry fields. In some places, groundwater has dropped by 20 metres (66 feet). Wildlife – especially freshwater wildlife – has suffered. This is because fresh groundwater which normally keeps flowing to the surface, keeping away the salt water from the sea, has been drained and can no longer act as a defence. So saltwater comes pushing in and the water life suffers.

Ladybird summer

In England in 1976, drought ruined crops and dried up reservoirs and dams. Many wild plants, birds and mammals died, but millions of ladybirds hatched out, producing black clouds that descended on tourists sunbathing on the south coast. The summer of 1976 became known as 'Ladybird summer'.

Without water this frog cannot reproduce, for the spawn needs to be laid in a pond or slow-moving river. More than this, the adult frog itself has to keep its thin skin moist by continually plunging into cool water. Like other amphibians, such as the newt, its skin actually absorbs oxygen from the water.

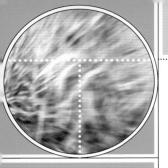

Collecting water

Is it enough?

Generally, a minimum of 300–400 millimetres (12–16 inches) of rain is needed every year for **arable** farming (crop-growing) to take place. In many parts of the world, this does not occur regularly. Sometimes the right amount of rain falls, but within a very short time, so that crops die before they have had time to grow properly and ripen. Then conserving water and **irrigating** the land have prevented drought. But as we shall see, irrigating land has its disadvantages.

Dams and drought

For thousands of years communities have controlled water sources such as rivers so that they can irrigate fields or stop flooding. Dams, which halt the natural flow of rivers, have been used across the world. The first dams were built from banks of clay or stone, with irrigation channels running from them to reservoirs or fields. Nowadays, huge concrete structures hold water not only for agricultural use but also for hydro-electric power, industry and for supplying water to big cities.

Saving water in this way seems like a good idea, except that water collected in huge modern dams **evaporates** very quickly. **Silt** no longer gets washed down with the floodwaters, so artificial fertilizers have to be used instead. These can eventually pollute **groundwater**, saturating it with chemicals. It puts no **humus** into the soil, either. Irrigation has also led to waterlogging, which raises the water table, bringing salts and alkalis nearer to plant roots. The new water channels also encourage the snail that brings the disease **bilharzia**, which is now widespread in Egypt.

Drought data

These are some irrigation methods, both ancient and modern:

- shaduf – an ancient method of irrigation using buckets to collect river water, which is then swung around to fill irrigation channels by the sides of fields.

- sakia (also known as Archimedes' screw) – another ancient method of irrigation which uses a large twisting screw inside a pipe to lift water.

- drip irrigation – a modern method using plastic pipes with small holes along the length, which allow water slowly to penetrate to plants' roots. It is very direct and wastes little water. Less water evaporates from the soil, too.

- boom irrigation – another modern method using a huge rotating sprinkler which creates large circles of damp soil in which to plant crops. It is often used in desert locations. Water tends to evaporate from the surface too quickly though.

Irrigation from Egypt's Aswan Dam has led to more crops being grown for export, such as cotton, citrus fruits, potatoes, maize and scented flowers for the perfume industry. Farmers have been able to earn cash, which is important in bad years.

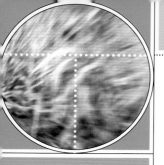

Water problems – and solutions

Draining water sources

Groundwater is used to water crops grown on the High Plains to the east of the Rocky Mountains in the United States, but groundwater often feeds springs, surface streams and marshland, which are lost when too much water is pumped up. This means that natural drought will have a greater impact – there will be fewer reserves of water. The world's marshlands are continually being drained to provide water for agriculture, industry and growing cities. This not only affects rich wildlife habitats, but destroys the delicate **ecosystem**. The destruction of marshland can lead to drought conditions on the margins of **wetlands**, which have no means of recovering.

Saving the delta

The Okavango Delta in Botswana is a huge area of low-lying swamp and rivulets fed by the Okavango River. It is surrounded by semi-desert. The waters cover 16 000 square kilometres (6200 square miles) during the rainy season, reducing to about half when it is dry. Botswana's Department of Water had planned to take water out of the delta, to fill dams which could **irrigate** fields for growing **cash-crops**. The local farmers, including many who the project was intended to help, protested. They said that draining part of the delta would in fact destroy it, leading to disastrous drought conditions on their farmlands. The Botswanan Government called in the International Union for the Conservation of Nature and Natural Resources (IUCN) which discovered that the soil was not actually suitable for cash-crop agriculture.

The IUCN's scientists also agreed that taking water from the delta would indeed dry up the small farmers' pastures and fields, so it would not help them at all. The Botswanan Government bravely decided to change its mind, and implement the IUCN's recommendations. The delta was saved.

Let the river flow!

River channels are often straightened and lined with concrete to make water transport easier, but a river flows much faster in a straight line, and this badly erodes the river bed. It leads to a fall in the water level and a fall in the groundwater in the land surrounding the river. Crops, natural plants and animals die as they are left high and dry. The Missouri River in the United States was once a shallow haven for marshland birds such as the piping plover. Its width varied between 600 and 1800 metres (2000–6000 feet), but it was dammed and channelled so that its course deepened and narrowed to just 180 metres (600 feet) at is widest point. This created a fast, straight course for shipping but destroyed the marshland habitat.

In the 1960s a straight canal was made which stopped the Kissimee River from winding its way through the swamp, feeding it with water. Now, 35 kilometres (22 miles) of canal is being changed back into 69 kilometres (43 miles) of natural, meandering river like this one, in the hope of restoring the swamps.

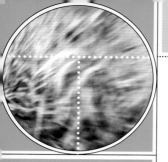

Measuring drought

Meteorologists and other scientists use many tools to predict short-term weather conditions. In well-known drought-stricken areas in the developing world, most communities are used to surviving even several years of drought. Here, drought disaster is only a certainty when there is no more grain in the grainstores to either eat or plant, and when animals have had to be sold to buy food. This might happen quite suddenly during a particularly bad year. In these conditions, short-term weather predictions are usually too late to save crops, animals and human life. But in these poor parts of the world, daily and monthly measurement of different moisture levels help to alert governments and aid agencies, so that communities can receive help and disaster is avoided.

The tools of the trade

Digital satellite images from different periods are compared to show where areas of the world have lost their greenness. They also show where lakes have **evaporated**. These pictures are used with predictions of long-term climate change and the measurements listed below to give at least a three-month drought warning.

The amount of a particular crop harvested during a season is called its yield. Crop yields are measured to find out if they have been affected by drought, and to give an idea of what will happen the following year if the rain fails.

Drought data

These are some of the ways in which drought is measured:

- **Precipitation** – the amount of rainfall and dew. Rainfall total is measured on a monthly basis and is compared with expected rainfall levels. Dry periods in between rain are measured, too.

- Run-off – the amount of running water or streamflow.

- **Groundwater** – the amount of water available under ground.

- Soil moisture – the levels of water in the soil.

- Evaporation – the amount of moisture from the ground that is heated up by the sun to form water vapour, which rises into the atmosphere. It is measured using a pan called an evaporimeter, which is filled with water. Evaporimeters are all exactly the same size and shape.

- **Evapotranspiration** – the amount of moisture lost from the ground (evaporation) added to the amount of moisture lost through tiny holes, called **stomata**, in plant leaves.

- Humidity – the amount of water vapour in the air.

Alice Springs is in the Simpson Desert, a **semi-arid** region of central Australia. Many sheep and cattle are raised on the vast, drought-prone pastures here. Scientists in the region measure drought on a daily basis.

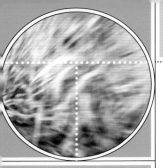

Why live in danger?

People have adapted to living in dry conditions, and even long periods of drought, but why do people live in drought disaster zones?

More than just survival

Over hundreds of years, people have developed ways of life and rich cultures in drought-prone areas throughout the world. The western **Sahel** is a good example. It lies between forests to the south and desert to the north. For centuries merchants from the Sahel traded goods from the forest with those from the desert and North Africa. Trading cities that grew up in these **semi-arid** parts are still there today. As well as this, the Sahel has provided pasture for **nomadic** herdsmen. In normal seasons it is good grain-growing country, too, and in the long dry season, craft manufacturing takes place. In normal conditions, the Sahel is a productive place, but lack of seasonal rainfall, a rapid increase in population, **overgrazing** and deforestation have made parts of it into a disaster zone.

The Khoikhoi of the Kalahari in Africa are able to find water in a seemingly parched landscape. These Khoikhoi women are collecting water from a hidden underground spring.

Shortage in the cities

Rapid increases in industry and urban populations create strains on national water supplies. The highly-populated Chinese capital, Beijing, and the Mexican capital, Mexico City have hovered on the brink of drought disaster in recent years. Beijing has suffered not only because of a rapid increase in population but also because it has used the dry countryside around the capital for intensive agriculture. This has diverted water supplies which could have been used by city dwellers and industry.

Drought data

Drought itself is a natural occurrence, but a drought disaster zone can be made by humans almost anywhere. Below are other factors which can make a disaster likely, if accompanied by a phase of unusually dry weather.

- Soil erosion and water loss through deforestation, overgrazing, land clearance and forest or bush fire.

- Single-crop cultivation, especially where that crop is not drought-resistant.

- Lack of industry and no service sector in the economy to provide wage-earning jobs. A family needs to earn cash to buy food in times of drought.

- A seasonal food supply – an all-year-round supply is required.

- Inefficient methods of food production.

- Weak transport and distribution systems.

- Poor transport links to the local area.

- Governments unable to forecast and respond to disaster.

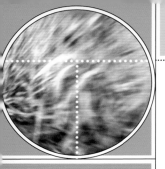

Food aid and foreign attitudes

Drought disaster leads to famine and a desperate cry for help. Over half of all food aid is usually given by the drought-stricken countries themselves, however poor they may be. In Ethiopia in the 1980s, it was the Ethiopian Red Cross that gave the largest single contribution to those suffering – not foreign governments or aid agencies. Food aid often comes too late. Governments in poor parts of the world are often slow to predict disaster and to respond to it. They simply do not have the resources to keep track of what is happening. Governments are often slow and reluctant to ask for help, particularly if there is a war taking place. International aid agencies can be slow, too, and their relationship with governments is sometimes uneasy. There are often so many aid agencies in one place that too much time is spent organizing them – the victims have to wait.

Aid convoys like this can provide food to help people recover from drought disaster, but aid has not always met people's needs. Foreign aid in the past has proved to be just a way for some foreign governments and huge corporations to dump unwanted food and equipment.

A survival guide

Most people need to eat enough food to provide at least 1500 kilocalories each day just to survive. When people eat less than this, their bodies suffer from undernourishment.

People need to eat a variety of foods. Protein, which helps the body to grow and to replace dead tissue, is found in meat, fish, milk products and pulses such as beans. Carbohydrates give energy and are found in cereals and root crops such as potatoes. When both of these are in short supply, the body loses weight and weakens. The victim often suffers from chronic diarrhoea, and **parasites** such as hookworm and roundworm take any nourishment left in the body. A shortage of vitamins can cause parts of the body to deteriorate and can cause blindness, skin disease and weakened bones. Undernourishment also reduces the body's resistance to other diseases. Children, especially, and the elderly, die from treatable conditions such as **malaria**, measles and chest infections.

Drought victims need not only food but also emergency shelter, a clean water supply and proper sanitation. This helps to avoid fatal diseases such as cholera, which is carried by **contaminated** water.

Immediate needs

The best type of aid starts by tackling the immediate problem, which is hunger and thirst, then tries to encourage long-term recovery by trying to give people a future free from disaster. The first line of attack is **oral rehydration** treatment, using is a liquid made up of water, salt and sugar in exact proportions. This can often save people on the brink of death, but it has to be followed by a protein and carbohydrate-rich diet supplying at least 2000 kilocalories a day. At the same time, victims should be immunized against disease, which increases when people are crammed together in huge feeding camps.

Planning for the future

Large-scale food aid is only the first step to helping people in a natural disaster. These are just some of the measures that are being put into place to help prevent drought disasters in the developing world.

Mixed solutions

- Drought-prone areas need people employed in industry. Industry provides people with cash to buy food from parts of the country not hit by drought.

- It is better if people work in a **co-operative** than trying to do it alone. Co-operatives are organizations of local people who share their labour and duties, and put back profits into the business.

- Markets set up in local towns can provide an outlet for goods manufactured in rural areas. International markets organized by aid agencies such as Oxfam also provide an important outlet.

- **Reforestation** can prevent soil erosion and preserve water. This is happening in the **Sahel**, but trees are still being felled faster than they are being replanted.

In the 1930s low rainfall, hot, dry winds and intensive farming caused a severe drought area known as the 'dust bowl' in the American midwest. In 1938 this farm in Texas looked more like a desert than agricultural land.

Drought data

Drought disasters do not only happen in developing countries. Other nations, such as the United States and Australia, have had to work out and practise some of these water conservation methods being practised in cities.

- Installing non-flushing or water-efficient flushing toilets
- Recycling waste water from homes and offices
- Collecting and reusing rainwater that runs into drains
- Metering and taxing water to discourage overuse
- Rationing water – only using it at certain times of the day
- Banning sprinklers – sprinkled water **evaporates** too quickly
- Planting drought-resistant plants and grasses

In some areas of the American Great Plains, **prairie** grasses are being reintroduced and bison are being returned to their native grounds. Eventually this will help neighbouring farmers by restoring some of the natural **ecosystem** of the area.

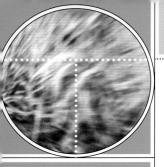

Drought in history

Drought and famine are disasters that have affected humans and the natural world for thousands of years. It is very difficult to prove how many people were affected in any single drought disaster. Even nowadays, the calculations are clouded by other factors. Famine may be caused not just by drought but by insect plagues and crop disease – although these, too, are often worsened by drought conditions. Drought makes plants weak and more likely to become diseased. It also makes them unable to produce new growth after insect attack. In terms of human deaths, disease often claims lives before hunger takes a real grip.

Drought data

These are some of the most tragic disasters of the past.

- One of the earliest recorded drought famines occurred in Rome in 436 BCE. Thousands of people drowned themselves rather than suffer the slow death of starvation and disease.

- In Europe during the Middle Ages a sudden warm weather phase occurred between 879 and 1162, causing failed crops, population migration and hundreds of thousands of deaths.

- India suffered three successive famines in late 18th century and eight in the late 19th century. Millions died.

This amazing art was created by the peoples who once inhabited a green, fertile Sahara. The type of animals depicted can no longer survive there.

Drought and faith

Stories of drought, plague, famine and migration feature strongly in ancient scriptures. The scriptures tell how **nomadic pastoralists** from **semi-arid** Palestine begged permission to enter the rich lands of Egypt when drought shrivelled their sparse grasslands. Egypt guarded its boundaries well – and Palestinian refugees required permits to enter the kingdom. There are ancient records of these permits, proving that the stories of drought refugees were based in truth. Dating these ancient drought disasters exactly is difficult. It has been made worse by the fact that many of the records from the Hyksos dynasty, during which they happened, were destroyed by the Egyptian rulers that followed. But enough records survive which agree with each other to show that the stories are true.

Palestine is a land that seems dry, rocky and inhospitable for most of the year. Rain is in fact plentiful, but it all falls within about six weeks. It can be so torrential that it runs off the hillsides without soaking into the soil. An ancient way of collecting the run-off was to dig channels down the hillsides. These led to wells or huge underground stores made of stone. This Palestinian farmer is cultivating his rocky, hillside terraces.

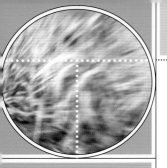

Disastrous droughts

Dreadful drought disasters

These are some of the most devastating drought disasters that we know of, in chronological order (starting from long ago and ending with recent times). Some of these disasters were made worse by warfare and disease, and it is difficult to separate out these calamities.

Date	Place	Number of deaths
436 BCE	Rome	Thousands
1586	England	Thousands
610 drought years in the period 610–1619	parts of China	Millions
1692–94	France	2 000 000
1708–1711	East Prussia	250 000
1890s – eight drought years in succession	India	Millions
1876–1879	China	9–13 000 000
1983–1985	Horn of Africa	500 000

In a normal year, 2000 tonnes of dust can fall over just 2.5 square kilometres (one square mile) of our largest cities. Dust clouds obviously increase as drought sets in. Strangely, without minute dust particles, we would have no mist, fog or rain clouds! Each speck forms a tiny centre – or nucleus – around which water vapour can **condense** to form rainclouds.

Humans start over 90 per cent of forest fires – usually through carelessness – but the worst fires happen in times of drought. 1998 was a very hot year in Australia, and forest fires broke out in five states. In New South Wales, they were fuelled by winds gusting at more than 110 kilometres per hour (68 miles per hour). At the same time, in Brazil, three dry months saw fires that burned an area of forest and farmland the size of Ireland.

Searching for past disasters

It is interesting that the list on page 44 shows no drought disasters in North and South America. These parts of the world do suffer from drought, but there is little evidence of great human catastrophe in these areas. We can find out more accurately when drought occurred in the past by using dendrochronology (measuring tree rings), and by studying soil layers and the layers in ice samples from ice-sheets. To find out if these periods of drought affected people, we also need to find human archaeological remains such as bodies and the tools and treasures people gathered around them. Together, these can show whether widespread death or mass-movement of populations took place at the same time as severe drought.

Glossary

alkaline a substance containing a large amount of alkali – soils containing very large amounts offer difficult growing environments for some plants

altitude the height of something, usually above sea level

aquifer drought drought occurring where there is a lack of groundwater

arable a type of farming in which crops are grown

arid very dry (land)

atmosphere the layers of gases that surround the Earth

bilharzia a disease transmitted to humans by worms that live as parasites inside water snails

carbon gases gases containing carbon, given off by burning fossil fuels such as coal, gas or oil

carcasses bodies of dead animals

cash-crop crops that can be sold rather than eaten

catchment area all the surface and underground water that runs into a single main river

CFCs chlorofluorocarbon gases, such as those found in many refrigerators

chernozem a fine, fertile block of dark brown soil rich in decayed vegetable matter (humus)

condense when water vapour (the gas form of water) is cooled so much that it changes into a water droplet

contaminate to pollute with bacteria

contingent drought a rainy season that is cut short, or which gives less rain than usual

co-operative a group of people who work together, sharing both the labour (work) and the profit (gain)

dengue fever a disease caused by a virus transmitted by mosquitoes

ecosystem a particular environment in which plants and animals live – also the relationship between these plants, animals and the climate

El Niño a weather phenomenon in which the direction of prevailing winds is reversed and ocean currents warm up causing violent changes in weather

evaporate turn into a vapour (gas)

evapotranspiration the total loss of water by evaporation and by water loss through plant leaves

glacier a huge, very thick area of ice

global warming the warming of the Earth's climate

greenhouse effect when layers of gases in the atmosphere reflect back the Sun's energy that the Earth is reflecting or radiating into space

groundwater the water lying in the soil and between underground rocks

halophyte a plant that is able to cope with salty conditions

hazard mapping mapping areas most likely to suffer from disaster

high pressure an area of dry, cool, descending air

humus broken-down plant matter

ice cap a very thick, permanent cap of ice on top of a mountain

ice sheet a very thick, permanent sheet of ice

Industrial Revolution a time in the late 17th century when factories and machinery began to mass-produce goods

infrastructure communications, transport and essential services, such as water supply, electricity, and drainage.

inter-cropping planting crops – such as beans and maize – between each other in the same field

invisible drought rainfall which is so weak, and occurs so seldom, that it harms crops and wildlife but does not completely destroy them

irrigation, irrigate keeping plants alive and healthy by artificial watering

loess a very fine, yellow, clay-like soil found in thick layers, especially in northern China

malaria a disease caused by parasites transmitted by mosquitoes

nitrate a chemical that helps to make soil more fertile

nomadic someone who travels with their family and belongings from one site to another – many are pastoralists

North Atlantic Oscillation (NAO) a change in air pressure and wind above the Atlantic, affecting weather in western Europe and North Africa

nutrients vitamins and minerals that help living things to grow

oral rehydration a treatment for severe malnutrition and diarrhoea, using water, salt and sugar

oscillation a sudden rise in temperature in the middle of a cold phase in the climate – or a sudden cooling down in the middle of a hot one

overgraze to allow animals to graze on one piece of pasture for too long, so that the grasses are unable to grow back

ozone layer a protective layer of the gas ozone lying high up above the Earth

parasite a living thing that attaches itself to another living thing, feeding off and taking strength from it

pastoral farming animal-rearing

pastoralist a farmer who herds animals – many are nomadic

permanent drought dry conditions found always in desert regions

plateau a high, flat stretch of land, often between two mountains

prairie a vast expanse of grassland

precipitation drought a drought caused by a lack of rain

precipitation rain, hail, snow or dew

prevailing wind a wind that blows continually in one direction

pyrophytic trees and plants that are resistant to fire

rainshadow area an area on one side a mountain which receives very little rainfall

reforestation replanting trees which have been cut down in a particular area

river basin the area of land in which all surface and underground water runs into a single main river

run-off drought drought caused by a lack of running water – such as dried-out rivers and streams

Sahel semi-arid area in Africa that lies between the desert and the forest

savannah natural grasslands in Africa and the Americas

seasonal drought conditions that are hot and dry for most of the year, broken by a short rainy season

semi-arid very dry conditions, but not quite desert

silt very fine soil deposited by rivers

stomata tiny holes in plants' leaves through which gases pass, including evaporating water

subsidy money given to farmers by the government to help them grow a particular crop, usually one that can be exported for cash

unpredictable drought humid weather conditions with sudden rainbursts

water cycle the way in which water is continually recycled in different forms – as water, hail, ice, snow or vapour (gas)

wetlands soggy marshland

xerophytic (pronounced 'zerofitic') a plant that is resistant to drought

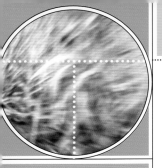

Index